CPSIA information can be obtained
at www.ICGtesting.com
Printed in the USA
LVHW071114231218
601526LV00016B/526/P

#8—My favorite day of the week is:

A Saturday, because I can skateboard to the movies.

B Friday, because I get to hang out at the mall.

C Monday, because I love school.

Write down your points! A=1, B=2, C=3.

#9—Rings are practical because:

A They give me something to play with while I wait for everyone else to finish their tests.

B I can make them for all of my friends.

C They can be worn on fingers, toes, and through the nose.

Write down your points! A=3, B=2, C=1.

#10—If I could go anywhere in the world, I'd go to:

I WONDER IF I CAN BE A BEAD MAJOR IN COLLEGE?

A Kenya to see amazing animals.

B France to see the Mona Lisa in the Louvre.

C Toronto—I hear it has great shopping.

Write down your points! A=1, B=3, C=2.

#11—I love my friends because:

A They are just as unique as I am.

B We work together as a team.

C They laugh at my jokes.

Write down your points! A=1, B=3, C=2.

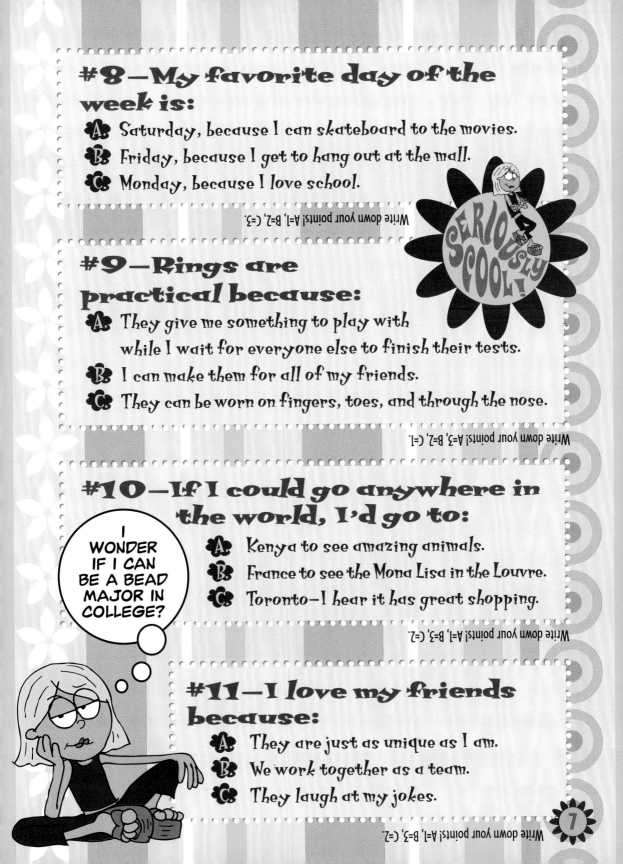

#12—During the winter I like to:

A Write poetry about the beauty of each individual snowflake.

B Identify animal tracks in the snow.

C Have friends over for hot chocolate and s'more parties.

Write down your points! A=1, B=3, C=2.

now total your quiz points.

If they total 29-36, you are the
Teacher's Pet!

You're class president—a super student and proud of it. Look out world—here you come!

If your points total 20-28, you are a
Party Animal!

If there's a party—you're there! You love a crowd of any kind, and you love to perform. You are sure to be a star!

If your points total 12-19, you are
One of a Kind!

People look to you to set the trend, even though you couldn't care less! You do things your own way—you're totally cool!

Each time you take the quiz, you may get a different score. That's OK 'cause that's just one of the cool things about being a girl! Now, find a beading project that matches your personality of the day and have a blast making everything from bracelets to lamps!

beading basics

beads of every kind

This sampling shows a few of the beautiful types of beads available for your projects. Bead and crafts stores offer beads that are made from glass, plastic, metal, wood, stones, and shells.

bugle beads

transparent seed beads

opaque glass beads

crystal beads

shaped cane-glass beads

bumpy glass beads

charms

two-color glass beads

leaf and flower glass beads

spacer beads

disk-glass beads

wire beads

9

beading basics

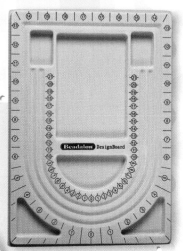

Bead Stringing Wire
This wire is very strong and is available in different sizes.

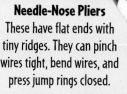

Elastic Cord
Created for making jewelry, this elastic is available in different sizes and comes in clear and limited colors.

Beading Tray
The plastic tray has measurement marks and channels to assist with bead arrangement. If a tray is unavailable, use a piece of felt to keep beads from rolling.

silver headpins

barrel clasps and jump rings

spring ring clasps

Round-Nose Pliers
These pliers grab wire allowing you to wrap it around the nose of the pliers. This forms spirals in the wire.

Needle-Nose Pliers
These have flat ends with tiny ridges. They can pinch wires tight, bend wires, and press jump rings closed.

Crimping Tool
This tool is used with crimping beads to hold them in place on beading wire or string (see the opposite page).

Wire Cutters
These sharp snippers cut a variety of wire sizes.

attaching a clasp

WHAT YOU NEED

Wire cutters; beading wire; crimp beads
Jewelry clasp; crimping tool

HERE'S HOW

1. Gather the supplies listed above. Cut the beading wire to the length instructed in the project directions.

crimp beads

2. Thread a crimp bead on one end of beading wire, pass wire through the end of the jewelry clasp, and run wire back through the crimp bead in the opposite direction as shown in Photo A. (**Note:** The crimping tool has two notches, one to flatten the crimp bead and one to round out the flattened crimp.) Flatten the crimp bead firmly with a crimping tool as shown in Photo B. Squeeze the crimp bead again to round out the bead. Trim the wire end with wire cutters.

3. After the wire is beaded, repeat Step 2 to attach the remaining piece of clasp.

finishing with knots

WHAT YOU NEED

Beading elastic or cord
Jewelry glue or clear fingernail polish

HERE'S HOW

1. Tie a knot (or several) in the elastic as shown in Photo C. Trim off extra elastic.

2. Put a drop of glue on the knot as shown in Photo D. Let the glue dry.

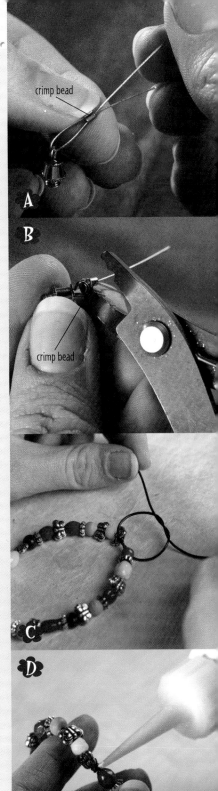

crimp bead

crimp bead

A

B

C

D

drop-dead gorgeous

You'll be a star when you wear a necklace that sings with color.

HANGIN' OUT

Beaded necklaces are the "in" thing, but add a nifty beaded teardrop—or three—and you'll have a necklace that is ...

Seriously Cool!

earth and sky trio choker (page 12)

WHAT YOU NEED

Beading wire; ruler

Three 2-inch silver headpins

Assorted beads for headpins; gold spacer beads

Six 5 mm gold accent beads; gold seed beads

Round-nose pliers

Beading tray (see page 10) or felt

Scissors; crimp beads; crimping pliers

Barrel clasp

HERE'S HOW

This is a 13-inch-long choker. Measure a piece of wire 13 inches long and see if you like the length. Add or subtract to the wire length as you wish.

1. Place assorted beads onto headpin, putting the larger beads at the bottom. Leave about $1/8$ inch of the headpin top free from beads. Fill two more headpins.

2. Use round-nose pliers to grip the end of the headpin wire and wrap it around until it makes a loop as shown in Photo A, opposite. Bend the loop until it forms a closed circle at the end.

3. Arrange headpins, seed, and spacer beads on a beading tray or felt to fill 13 inches. Begin at the 0 mark (center), where the center headpin will be, and arrange beads to $6\frac{1}{2}$ inches on each side. This choker has one headpin in the center with a gold spacer bead on each side, then eight seed beads, a spacer, a headpin, a spacer and enough seed beads to fill the $6\frac{1}{2}$-inch mark.

4. Cut a piece of wire 4 inches longer than the desired length. Thread a crimp bead on one end of beading wire, pass wire through the end of the clasp, and run wire back through the crimp bead in the opposite direction as shown on page 11, Photo A. Flatten the crimp bead firmly with a crimping tool as shown on page 11, Photo B. Squeeze crimp bead again to round out the bead. Trim the wire end with wire cutters.

I WONDER IF I COULD DO MY BEADING INSTEAD OF DRYING THE DISHES?

5 String beads in the arranged order. Attach the other end of the clasp, using the instructions in Step 4. Cut off extra wire.

❀ ❀ ❀

solo performer choker (page 13)

WHAT YOU NEED

2-inch silver headpin; assorted beads for headpin
Round-nose jewelry pliers
Beading tray (see page 10) or felt
Heart bead; assorted pink beads; silver seed beads
Four 5 mm silver spacer beads
Beading wire; scissors; barrel clasp
Crimp beads; crimping pliers

HERE'S HOW

This is a 13-inch-long choker. Measure a piece of wire 13 inches long and see if you like the length. Add or subtract to the wire length as you wish.

1 Place assorted beads onto headpin, putting the heart bead near the bottom. Leave about ⅛ inch of the headpin top free from beads.

2 Use round-nose pliers to grip the end of the wire and wrap it around until it makes a loop as shown in Photo A, above. Bend the loop until it forms a closed circle at the end.

3 Arrange the pink and silver beads onto a beading board or felt to fill 13 inches. Begin at the 0 mark (center), where the center

Ⓐ

headpin will be, and arrange beads to 6½ inches on each side. The choker on page 13 has one headpin in the center, silver spacer and pink beads, and about 5 inches of silver seed beads on the ends.

4 Cut a piece of wire 4 inches longer than the desired length. Thread a crimp bead on one end of beading wire, pass wire through the end of the clasp, and run wire back through the crimp bead in the opposite direction as shown on page 11, Photo A. Flatten the crimp bead firmly with a crimping tool as shown on page 11, Photo B. Squeeze crimp bead again to round out the bead. Trim the wire end with wire cutters.

5 String beads in the arranged order. Attach the other end of the clasp, using the instructions in Step 4. Cut off extra wire.

pure lizzie

Bake a cool clay necklace to wear with each of your favorite outfits.

HANGIN' OUT

Take your shirt with you to the beading store to match colors when you're picking out beads. That way, you'll be...

Seriously Cool!

pure lizzie continued

circles and squares necklace
(page 16)

WHAT YOU NEED

Waxed paper; polymer clay, such as Sculpey, in lime
   green, turquoise, and bright pink
Rolling pin; paper; ruler; pencil; scissors
Paring knife; paper clip; needle-nose pliers
Glass or metal baking dish; toothpick
4 small silver beads; oven; large silver jump ring
17-inch-long silver ball-chain necklace

HERE'S HOW

1 Place a piece of waxed paper on a flat work
   surface. Use your hands to knead one quarter
of the lime green clay square until it is pliable. Place
it on the waxed paper and
flatten slightly with
your palm.

> BIG NECKLACES MAKE ME FEEL SO POWERFUL!

2 Cover the clay piece with a second piece of
   waxed paper. Use a rolling pin to flatten the
clay until it is about $1/8$ inch thick as shown in Photo
A, opposite. Remove top piece of waxed paper.

3 Measure and mark a $1^{1}/_{2}$-inch square on
   paper and cut it out. Place the square on
the flattened clay. Use a paring knife to cut away
the clay around the square as shown in Photo B.

4 Use needle-nose pliers to bend a paper clip
   back and forth to break off a long U-shape
piece. Bend the ends back to create a hook as
shown in Photo C. Press the hooks into the green
clay square, placing the clip to stick out about
$1/8$ inch beyond one edge of the square. Roll two
tiny clay balls. Press the balls onto the back of the
square where the hooks enter the clay as shown in
Photo D. Carefully lift the square from the waxed
paper, turn it over, and place in a baking dish.

5 Place a marble-size piece of turquoise clay
   on the waxed paper. Using both hands, roll
it back and forth until a long, thin snake shape is
formed. Use the turquoise snake to border the
green square, cutting off the excess. Cut four
$1/4$-inch-long pieces from the snake excess as shown
in Photo E, page 21.

6 Shape four pea-size balls from pink clay.
   Flatten the balls as shown in Photo E, page 21.
Press a flattened ball on each side of the clay square.

7 Use a toothpick to make an indentation in
   the center of each pink circle. Lay a short

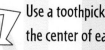

18

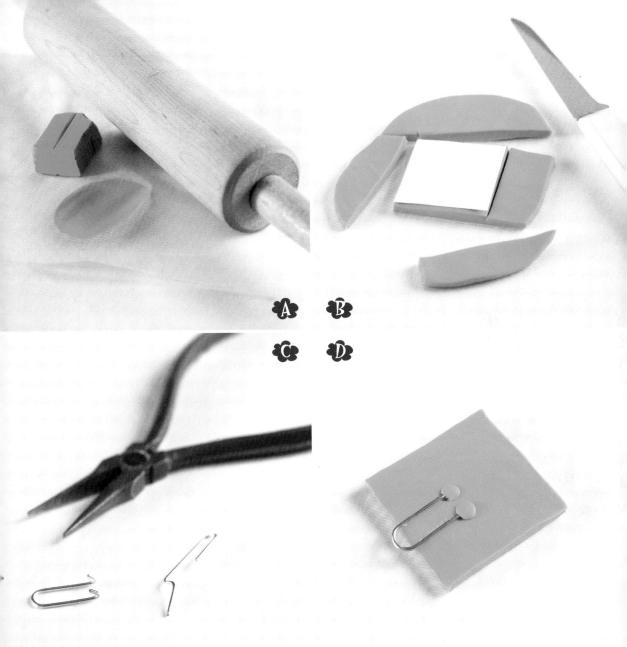

A **B**

C **D**

turquoise snake piece on each pink circle, extending from the indentation toward the center of the square.

8 Pick up a silver bead on the end of a toothpick. Place the bead in the indentation on the pink circle as shown in Photo F, page 21. Repeat for the remaining circles.

9 Bake the clay piece according to the clay manufacturer's directions. Let cool.

10 Use a jump ring and pliers to attach the pendant to the ball-chain necklace.

continued on page 20

adorable daisy necklace (page 17)

WHAT YOU NEED

Waxed paper
Polymer clay, such as Sculpey, in yellow and orange
Paring knife; needle-nose plier; paper clip
Baking dish; oven
Beading elastic
Large seed beads in red, orange, and yellow

HERE'S HOW

1. Place a piece of waxed paper on a flat work surface. Knead a small piece of yellow clay until pliable. Shape 12 small petals, each about $3/4$ inch long. Slightly flatten each petal shape. Use a knife to create an indentation on each petal as shown in Photo G, opposite.

2. Arrange the petals in a circle, pressing clay together slightly.

3. Use needle-nose pliers to bend a paper clip back and forth to break off a long U-shape piece. Bend the ends back to create hooks. Press the hook into petals, placing the clip about $1/8$ inch beyond the outer edge of the petals. Roll two tiny balls from yellow clay. Press the balls on the back of the petals where the hooks enter the clay. Carefully lift the circle of petals from the waxed paper, turn it over, and place in a baking dish.

4. Shape a grape-size ball from orange clay and flatten it slightly. Use a knife to make crossed lines in the flower center as shown in Photo H. Press into the center of the circle of petals.

5. Bake the clay piece according to the clay manufacturer's directions. Let cool.

6. Cut a 26-inch length of beading elastic. Fold the string in half. Slip the loop through the paper clip piece. Thread the ends of the string through the loop and pull tight to secure. String each side of the elastic in a pattern of red, orange, and yellow seed beads. Knot the ends together and trim off the excess.

I LOVE ROLLING OUT CLAY. IT MAKES ME WANT TO TAKE A COOKIE BREAK!

beads and buttons

have a heart bracelet

WHAT YOU NEED

Two 12-inch pieces of 1 mm clear elastic
Yellow and pink heart button with shank (loop
   on back); large seed beads in black and yellow
Tiny buttons in bright colors
Clear fingernail polish; scissors

HERE'S HOW

1 Slide both elastic pieces through the button shank. Center the button on the elastic pieces.

2 Thread yellow seed beads on both ends of one piece of elastic until you've reached the size you want.

3 On the second piece of elastic, thread four black seed beads on each side of the button. Thread on two small buttons, one on each side. Continue this pattern on both elastic ends until they're beaded the same length as the yellow seed beads.

4 Knot the elastic ends together. Dab the knot with fingernail polish and let dry. Trim the elastic ends.

HANGIN' OUT

Combine colorful plastic buttons and glass seed beads to make cute bracelets.

SCHOOL'S COOL

puppy power bracelet

WHAT YOU NEED

12-inch piece of 1 mm
   clear elastic
3 shank-style puppy
   buttons
Assorted glass beads
White glue
Scissors

shank buttons

HERE'S HOW

1 Slide the elastic through the hole in one of the puppy buttons and slide it to the center.

2 Thread 1½ inches of glass beads on each side of the button. Add a button to each end.

3 Thread more glass beads until you've reached the size you want.

4 Knot the ends together. Dab the knot with white glue and let dry. Trim the elastic ends.

23

luster lamps

Trim your favorite lamp with circles, fringe, and swirls–all made of glittering beads!

SCHOOL'S COOL

Pick up your homework–or a magazine about your favorite stars–and read by a light that's...

Seriously Cool

luster lamps continued

fringed-shade lamp (page 24)

WHAT YOU NEED

Small lamp with shade; assorted beads
Elastic cord; scissors; strong adhesive, such as E6000
Toothpick; silver spacer beads; seed beads
Beaded trim for shade; beading string
1 large heart bead

HERE'S HOW

1 String assorted beads onto elastic cord, and fit around lamp base. Tie the ends together in at least two knots and trim off the extra.

2 Use a toothpick to place dabs of adhesive around the base of the lamp. Press in silver spacer beads. Using a dab of adhesive, place a bead in the center of the silver spacer bead.

3 Cut beaded trim to the exact length needed to fit your lampshade. Spread a generous amount of adhesive onto the edge of the shade with a toothpick. Press the beaded trim onto the shade. Let dry.

4 The heart trim is hooked onto the inside of the shade. Cut a 12-inch piece of elastic. Tie a large bead on one end of the elastic. Thread about an inch of seed beads. Thread the elastic into the bottom of the heart bead. Add enough seed beads to go inside the shade, hook around the frame and back down to the heart bead and back through it. Thread another inch of seed beads and finish off with another end bead. Tie at least two or three knots on the end bead. Trim off extra string.

5 Cut a piece of elastic 2 inches longer than the top of the shade. String enough seed beads to fit around the shade; knot the ends. Trim off excess.

BEADS MAKE EVERYTHING BRIGHTER!

dots-all-around lamp (page 25)

WHAT YOU NEED

Table lamp with flat base
Double-stick tape for bead crafting
Scissors; marking pen
Small, round cups or lids
White glue; paintbrush
Tiny seed beads
Bugle beads
Strong adhesive, such as E6000

A

B

C

Black disk beads (available at crafts and
  beading stores); large seed beads
Medium weight beading wire

HERE'S HOW

1 Place a piece of double-stick tape around
  base of lamp. Sprinkle beads on tape until it is
well-covered.

2 Place cups or lids on the base of the lamp
  and use a marking pen to draw around them.

3 Paint a generous amount of white glue in
  the circles, as shown in Photo A, above.

4 Sprinkle seed beads onto the wet glue as
  shown in Photo B. Let dry. Shake off extra.

5 Place small dabs of strong adhesive onto
  the areas where you want to place beads
on the shade. Press the black disk beads in first as
shown in Photo C. Press the large seed beads into
the center. Let dry.

6 Cut a 14-inch piece of wire. Place a large
  seed bead on wire end; twist to secure.
String seed beads onto the wire. Tie a large seed
bead on the end. Trim off the extra wire. Wrap the
wire around the stem of the lamp.

think pink

sparkle and shine necklace

WHAT YOU NEED

Beading tray (see page 10) or felt

Set of long black beads in different lengths; scissors

Large pink seed beads

Large silver beads

Round black beads

Beading string; barrel clasp

Clear nail polish; beading needle

HERE'S HOW

1 Place the longest black bead on the 0 mark (center) on the beading tray. Place a silver bead and two pink beads on each side of the long black beads as shown. Arrange black beads from the longest to the shortest until the 9-inch marks are reached. Thread the tails with round black beads spaced with two pink seed beads.

2 Cut a 28-inch piece of string. Tie an end to a barrel clasp; knot several times leaving a 2-inch tail.

3 Paint a dot of nail polish on the knot and on the double threads; stick them together. Let dry.

4 Thread the string onto a needle. String with the beads on the tray.

5 Tie the string end to the clasp. Trim extra string to 2 inches and push it back into the beads if you can. Paint a dot of nail polish on the knot. Let the polish dry.

SCHOOL'S COOL

Throw on a scoop-neck top so you can show off your nifty necklaces!

HANGIN' OUT

pretty pastels necklace

WHAT YOU NEED

Beading tray (see page 10) or felt
½-inch-long flat pink beads; silver leaf-shape beads
Assorted pastel seed and pearl beads; scissors
Beading string; ruler; barrel clasp; beading needle
Clear nail polish

HERE'S HOW

1 Place a flat pink bead on the 0 mark (center) on the beading tray. Using the photo for ideas, arrange beads however you wish until you reach a 9-inch mark on each side.

2 Cut a 28-inch piece of string. Tie one end to the barrel clasp; knot, leaving a 2-inch tail.

3 Paint a dot of nail polish on the knot and on the double threads; stick them together. Let dry.

4 Thread the loose end of the string onto a needle. String the thread with beads.

5 Tie the other end of string onto the other end of the barrel clasp. Tie several knots. Trim extra string to 2 inches and push it back into the beads if you can. Paint a small dot of nail polish on the knot. Let the polish dry.

29

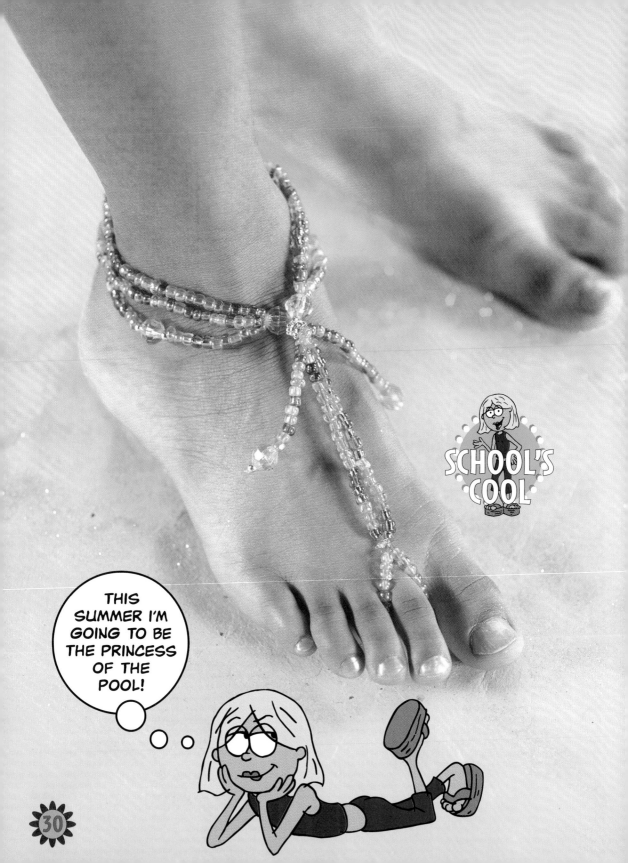

fancy foot bands

String your favorite colors of beads together to make snazzy foot jewelry.

HANGIN' OUT

fancy foot bands continued

pearled pinkies and blue-green beauty (pages 30-31)

WHAT YOU NEED

Ruler; scissors; .5 mm or 1 mm beading elastic cord
(Heavier is better as long as it fits through beads.)
Tape; small assorted beads such as pearls and
faceted pastel beads (see pages 30-31 for ideas)
3 spacer beads with large enough holes to fit
several elastic strands; seed beads

HERE'S HOW

Note: The directions for both foot bands are the
same, using whichever beads you prefer. You can
adjust the lengths of bead strands as you work to fit
your foot.

1. Cut three 24-inch-long pieces of elastic cord.
Place a piece of tape on one end of each
elastic piece to keep beads from falling off.

2. On one piece of elastic, string $4\frac{1}{4}$ inches
with beads, then add a large-holed spacer
bead. (The size should fit around your ankle
without drooping. You can make it larger or smaller
to fit.) String on another $4\frac{1}{4}$ inches of beads and
end with another spacer bead. Pull the elastic end
with no spacer bead through the spacer bead only
on the opposite end of elastic. (See Drawing A.)

3. Tie the two ends of the elastic together in
several tight knots around the spacer

bead. Trim off the extra cord. You now have a
single-strand anklet with spacer beads on each end.
The spacer with the knot will go in the front; the
other will be worn at your heel. (See Drawing B.)

4. Insert a second piece of elastic through the
spacer bead at the heel, leaving equal
amounts on both sides. String beads until you have
about 5 inches of beads strung. Pull the elastic ends
through the front spacer bead and tie around the
spacer bead with several
knots. Do not cut this
cord; leave two equal
tails. Bead 3 inches of
each tail and tie several
knots right after the
last bead until the knot is
big enough to hold beads
in place. Trim off extra cord.
(See Drawing C.)

5. Insert a third piece
of elastic through
the spacer bead at the heel,
leaving equal amounts on both ends.
String $5\frac{1}{2}$ inches of beads onto each
cord end. Pull each end through the
front spacer bead and knot around
the bead. (See Drawing D.)

6. Try on your anklet to see how
it fits and how long you need

> WEARING BEADED FOOT BANDS MAKES ME FEEL LIKE A QUEEN!

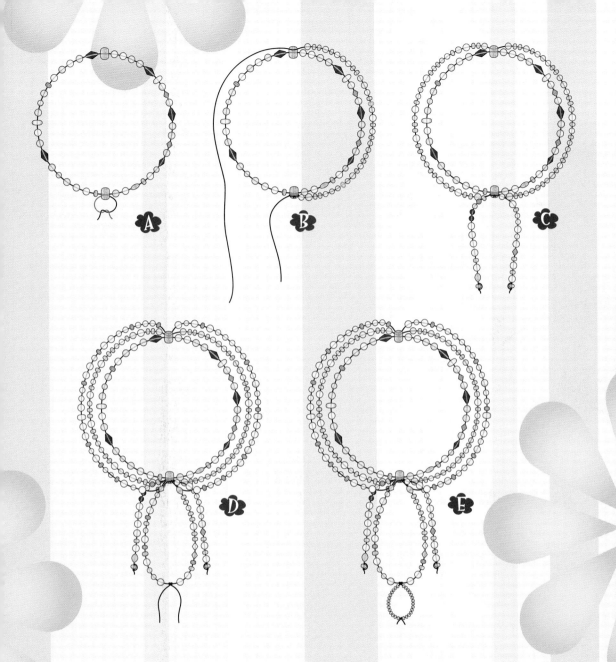

to make the beaded cord that will reach your second toe. It probably will be 1 to 2½ inches. String beads onto each loose tail to reach the desired length and knot the ends together several times. To make the toe loop, string about 1¼ inches

of seed beads onto one elastic end. (See Drawing E.) Knot the strands together several times. Make sure the knots are secure before trimming off the extra cord.

chic chandelier earrings

berry bobbles

WHAT YOU NEED

6 headpins; assortment of beads
Round-nose pliers; chandelier form (available in
 crafts and bead stores)
Jump rings; ear wires

HERE'S HOW

1 For each earring, thread beads onto three
 headpins, placing larger beads on the bottom.
Make the center headpin longer, as shown. Leave
1/4 inch of headpin without beads.

2 Use round-nose pliers to grip the end of
 one beaded headpin and curl it over,
making a loop to hold
the beads in place.
Squeeze it closed. Repeat
for two other headpins.

3 Use pliers to
 open three
jump rings. Hook one
onto each loop of the
headpin. Hook rings onto
the chandelier form and
close them with pliers.
Hook a bead to the top
of the chandelier.

4 Use a jump
 ring to connect
the ear wire to the
chandelier form.

SCHOOL'S
COOL

Thread tiny beads on headpins to create these clever, "in" earrings.

HANGIN' OUT

ocean blue

WHAT YOU NEED

6 headpins; assortment of beads
Round-nose pliers
Chandelier forms (available in crafts and bead stores)
Jump rings; ear wires

chandelier forms

HERE'S HOW

1 For each earring, thread beads onto three headpins, placing larger beads on the bottom. Make the one in the center longer as shown above. Leave $1/4$ inch of headpin without beads.

2 Use round-nose pliers to grip the end of one beaded headpin wire and curl it over, making a loop so the beads will not fall off. Squeeze it closed. Repeat for two other headpins.

3 Use the pliers to open three jump rings. Hook one onto each loop of the headpin. Hook rings onto the chandelier form and close them with pliers. Hook a bead to the top of the chandelier.

4 Use a jump ring to connect the ear wire to the chandelier form.

35

HANGIN' OUT

CHECK OUT PAGES 40-41. YOU CAN MAKE NECKLACES TO MATCH YOUR SHIRTS!

fun flower shirts and chains

SCHOOL'S COOL

Use the colorful iron-on designs in the back of this book to make a floral T-shirt!

There are a zillion kinds of shirts, but the ones you make—especially those with sweeet beaded trims—are so ...

Seriously cool!

fun flower shirts continued

bright blue blooms

WHAT YOU NEED

Turquoise V-neck T-shirt (50% cotton/50% polyester works best); 1 yard turquoise and green beaded trim; scissors; fabric glue; iron; jar lids Bead glue; blue-green seed beads
Iron-on flowers from the pages following the index

HERE'S HOW

1 Cut a short length of beaded trim to fit the right side of the T-shirt neckline. Cut a long piece of trim that reaches from the left neckline to the bottom right side of the shirt.

2 Glue the beaded pieces to the shirt using fabric glue. Let the glue dry.

3 Remove the flower iron-on pages. To cut circles around the shapes, trace around a jar lid that is bigger than the design.

4 Using the photo, below left, as a guide, place the iron-ons right-side down on the shirt. Ask an adult to slowly iron the back of the designs on high for no more than 1 minute, keeping the iron moving and avoiding the beads as shown in Photo A, opposite. Let the iron-ons cool; lift off the paper backing.

5 Spread bead glue in the center of the large iron-on flower. Sprinkle with seed beads as shown in Photo B. Let dry. Shake off the extra beads.

EVEN MIRANDA DOESN'T BELIEVE I MADE MY COOL SHIRT!

38

pink and yellow posies

WHAT YOU NEED

Green T-shirt (50% cotton/50%
   polyester works best); 1 yard pink
   beaded trim; scissors; fabric glue
Jar lids; iron; iron-on flowers from the pages
   following the index; bead glue; pink seed beads

HERE'S HOW

1 Cut beaded trim to fit shoulder seams
   and around sleeve hems. Glue the trim
pieces to the shirt using fabric glue. Let dry.

2 Remove the iron-on pages. To cut
   circles around the shapes, trace a
lid that is bigger than the design. Place the iron-ons
right-side down across the shirt front. Ask an adult
to slowly iron the back of the designs on high for no
more than 1 minute, keeping the iron moving and
avoiding the beads as shown in Photo A. Let cool.

3 Spread bead glue in the center of the
   large flower; sprinkle with seed beads
as shown in Photo B. Let dry. Shake off the
extra beads.

39

fun flower chains

WHAT YOU NEED

40-inch piece of beading wire

Beading needle

Barrel or spring ring clasp

Size 11/0 seed beads in green, blue, and yellow
or pink, orange, red, and lime green with silver
bugle beads

HERE'S HOW

1 Thread the needle onto the piece of wire. Tie one end of the barrel clasp to one end of the wire, knotting so that the clasp will not come off.

2 To make the first daisy, put on four "petal" seed beads. Next put on one "center" seed bead as shown in Diagram A, opposite. Put the needle back through the first bead and pull tight as shown in Diagram B.

3 Put on two more petal beads as shown in Diagram C. Put the needle back through the petal bead next to the center bead as shown in Diagram D. Pull thread tight to make a daisy as shown in Diagram E.

4 Thread on eight green seed beads or two silver bugle beads with a seed bead between them.

5 Repeat Steps 2-4 until the chain is long enough to make a necklace. Tie the clasp on the other end.

SCHOOL'S COOL

MAYBE I'LL MAKE LONG DAISY CHAINS TO COVER MY BEDROOM DOOR.

HANGIN' OUT

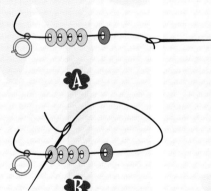

A

B

C

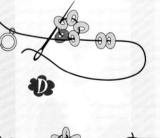

D

E

charms all around

all-girl collection bracelet

WHAT YOU NEED

Beading tray (see page 10) or felt; pink beads
Silver spacer beads; charms
Elastic cord; ruler; scissors; tape; crafts glue

HERE'S HOW

1 Design a bead pattern for the bracelet. Using the photo for ideas, lay the beads and charms in order on a beading tray until about 7 inches is filled.

2 Cut a 12-inch-long piece of elastic cord. Place a piece of tape on one end to keep beads from sliding off while working.

3 String the beads and charms onto the elastic until a length is reached to fit your wrist. Tie the elastic ends until the beads meet. Tie several knots until very secure. Cut off the ends. Put a dot of glue on the knot; let dry.

HANGIN' OUT

46

Mix in whimsical charms with a beaded pattern to make bracelets with a theme.

timeless design bracelet

WHAT YOU NEED

Beading tray (see page 10) or felt
Gold spacer beads
Black beads; charms
Elastic cord; ruler
Scissors; tape

HERE'S HOW

1 Design a bead pattern for the bracelet. Using the photo for ideas, lay the beads and charms in order on a beading tray until about 7 inches is filled.

2 Cut a 12-inch piece of cord. Tape one end to keep beads from sliding off.

3 String the beads and charms onto the elastic until a length is reached to fit your wrist. Tie the elastic ends until the beads meet. Tie several knots until very secure. Cut off the ends. Put a dot of glue on the knot; let dry.

47

so-cute cuffs

Use double-stick tape to hold a sprinkling of seed beads on a bright foam cuff.

Even when I don't have a ton of free time, I can still make fun and trendy cuff-style bracelets that are...

Seriously cool!

49

so-cute cuffs continued

tickled pink (page 48)

WHAT YOU NEED

Ruler; pencil; pink crafting foam, such as Fun Foam
Decorative-edge scissors; paper punch
Double-stick peel-off tape; assorted seed beads
16-inch piece of $1/2$-inch-wide ribbon; scissors
Needle and thread; large decorative bead

HERE'S HOW

1 Use a pencil to measure and mark a 2×6$3/4$-inch rectangle on foam.

2 Cut out the rectangle using decorative-edge scissors.

3 Measure in $3/4$ inch from a long edge and mark eight spots $3/4$ inch apart.

WHY STOP AT MY WRISTS? I'M MAKING AN ANKLE CUFF TOO!

4 Use a paper punch to punch holes on the markings as shown in Photo A, opposite.

5 Place double-stick tape along each long edge of foam, allowing the decorative edge to show. Peel off the protective strips on the tape as shown in Photo B.

6 Sprinkle seed beads onto the tape until well covered. Shake off the extra beads.

7 Starting from one end on the right side of the cuff, weave ribbon through the punched holes. Adjust the ribbon so it is even on each end of the cuff. Trim the ends neatly.

8 Use a needle and thread to sew a bead to the center of your cuff.

groovy green (page 49)

WHAT YOU NEED

Ruler; pencil; green crafting foam, such as Fun Foam
Decorative-edge scissors; paper punch
Double-stick peel-off tape
Assorted seed beads
16-inch piece of $1/2$-inch-wide ribbon
Scissors
Shank-style button

shank buttons

A B

HERE'S HOW

1 Use a pencil to measure and mark a 2×6³/₄-inch rectangle on foam.

2 Cut out the rectangle with decorative-edge scissors.

3 Measure in ³/₄ inch from a long edge and mark eight spots ³/₄ inch apart.

4 Use a paper punch to punch holes on the markings as shown in Photo A.

5 Place double-stick tape along each long edge of foam, allowing the decorative edge to show. Place short pieces of tape between the punched holes, connecting them to the long strips. Peel off the protective strips on the tape as shown in Photo B.

6 Sprinkle seed beads on the tape until well covered. Shake off the extra beads.

7 Starting from one end on the right side of the cuff, weave ribbon through the punched holes. After four holes are woven, thread the ribbon through the shank on the button. Continue weaving the ribbon through the foam cuff. Adjust the ribbon so it is even on each end of the cuff. Trim the ends neatly.

bright bobble chokers

Available in lots of colors, polymer clay can be shaped into beads and pendants.

HANGIN' OUT

Shaped by hand or cut with a cookie cutter, clay shapes you bake make happenin' accents for jewelry that's...

Seriously Cool

terrific triangle (page 52)

WHAT YOU NEED

Waxed paper; polymer clay, such as Sculpey, in
aqua, red, and yellow; rolling pin
Decorative-edge scissors; thin paintbrush handle
Toothpick; assorted bugle, seed, and pony beads
Decorative silver bead; glass baking dish; oven
Silver spacer beads; necklace wire

HERE'S HOW

1 Place waxed paper on a flat surface. Knead
clays until soft. To make red and aqua triangles,
roll out the clays to about $3/16$ inch thick. Cut out a
2-inch-high triangle from the red clay. Place the red
triangle on the aqua clay, pressing firmly without
damaging the shape. Cut a slightly larger aqua
triangle as shown in Photo A, opposite.

2 Lay a thin paintbrush handle on the top
end of the triangle. Fold the top corner
over and press a small ball of yellow clay onto the
tip as shown in Photo B. Press a decorative silver
bead into the yellow ball.

3 Press seed and bugle beads firmly into the
clay using the photo on page 52 as a guide.

4 Roll red and yellow clay into balls and disks.
Using a toothpick, poke holes in the balls
and disks, making sure they are big enough to
go onto the wire. Press beads into clay.

5 Place clay pieces on a baking dish. Have an
adult help you bake them according to the
manufacturer's instructions. Let cool.

6 Unscrew the ball from the necklace wire.
Slide on the beads. Screw on the ball end.

a trio of hearts (page 53)

WHAT YOU NEED

Polymer clay, such as Sculpey, in two shades each of
hot pink, yellow, orange, and green; oven
Rolling pin; heart-shape cookie cutter; toothpick
Assorted bugle and seed beads; glass baking dish
Gold and green beads; beading wire; necklace wire

HERE'S HOW

1 Knead clays until soft. Roll a piece of each of
the pink clays into a long shape, then roll and
twist together to get a marbled look. Do the same
with yellow, orange, and green.

2 For the pink hearts, roll the clay out flat and
cut out with a cookie cutter as shown in
Photo C, opposite. Roll two pea-size balls from
yellow clay and one from green. Press each onto the
top of a heart. Shape a yellow square bead. Insert a
toothpick and press seed beads into the clay.

3 Press the seed and bugle beads into the
clay firmly as shown in Photo D.

54

A   B

C   D

4   Using a toothpick, make holes in the clay balls and the square, making sure they are large enough for wire to fit through. Place clay pieces on a baking dish. Have an adult help you bake the clay pieces in the oven according to manufacturer's instructions. Let cool.

5   Use beading wire to attach the square clay bead to the green ball by winding it through the holes. Hide the ends inside the bead.

6   Unscrew the necklace wire ball. Slide on beads. Screw on the ball end.

55

so-simple belts

say it with silver

WHAT YOU NEED

Silver belt with rivets; strong adhesive, such as E6000
Pearl micro beads
Blue and purple mix of small glass beads

HERE'S HOW

1 Decide which belt rivets you would like to trim with beads. Keep the belt ends free of beads so the belt will buckle easily.

2 Working one rivet at a time, squeeze a wide ring of adhesive around the rivet. Sprinkle with micro beads. On the next rivet, use glass beads.

3 Continue gluing beads (switching types) around the rivets. Let the glue dry.

SCHOOL'S COOL

Make a belt frilly or flashy by gluing on beaded accents.

blooming garden

WHAT YOU NEED

Pink belt; strong adhesive, such as E6000
Plastic flower and leaf beads with flat backs
Metallic gold micro beads

HERE'S HOW

1 This belt is worn with the buckle to the side. If you pull the belt through belt loops, be careful, the beads may break off. Keep the belt ends free of beads so the belt will buckle easily.

2 Try on the belt with the buckle to the side. The section of the belt that is in the front is the part that should be decorated.

3 Arrange and glue flower beads on the front of the belt. Glue leaf beads near and under the flower petals.

4 Place a dot of adhesive in the center of each flower bead. Sprinkle with micro beads. Let dry.

HANGIN' OUT

two-cord creations

Suspend glass beads on cording with easy-to-do crimping.

Beading is always fun—but once you learn how to use crimping beads, you can add an artistic touch that's... *Seriously Cool!*

glass bead parade (page 58)

WHAT YOU NEED

Black leather cord thin enough to fit crimp beads

Ruler; scissors; decorative glass beads

Small round solid-color glass beads

Crimp bead; crimping pliers; barrel clasp

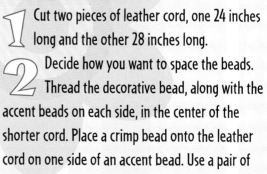

> AT LAST! A TOOL I CAN USE THAT I DON'T HAVE TO SNEAK FROM DAD'S WORKSHOP!

HERE'S HOW

1 Cut two 18-inch pieces of leather cord.

2 For each cord, decide how you want to space the beads. Lace a crimp bead onto the leather cord where you want the first bead. Use a pair of crimping pliers to squeeze the bead until it smashes and will not move on the cord as shown in Photo A, opposite.

3 Add a small round bead, a decorative bead, and another small round bead, or make any pattern you wish. Add another crimp bead close to the last bead and crimp it. Crimp beads hold the beads in place on the cord. Continue adding beads in this fashion until you have as many bead groups on the cord as you want.

4 Tie all four ends to the barrel clasp. Trim off the extra cord.

pretty as a pendant (page 59)

WHAT YOU NEED

Black leather cord thin enough to fit crimp beads

Scissors

Decorative glass bead

Small round solid-color glass beads

Crimp beads; crimping pliers; barrel clasp

HERE'S HOW

1 Cut two pieces of leather cord, one 24 inches long and the other 28 inches long.

2 Decide how you want to space the beads. Thread the decorative bead, along with the accent beads on each side, in the center of the shorter cord. Place a crimp bead onto the leather cord on one side of an accent bead. Use a pair of crimping pliers to squeeze the bead until it smashes and will not move on the cord as shown in Photo A, right. Place another crimp bead on the other side of the second glass bead, then squeeze it so that the three beads will not slide on the cord.

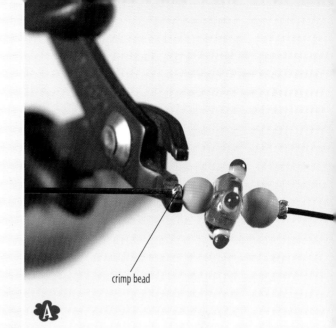

crimp bead

3 Tie the barrel clasp onto each end of the cord so that it will measure about 18 inches with the large bead at the center. Trim off the extra cord.

4 For the longer cord, arrange single beads onto one-half of the cord and add a crimp bead on each side so they will not move. Add a section of small beads in the center of the cord and keep them in place with a crimp bead on each side. Add single beads and crimp beads on the other half of the cord. See the photo on page 58 as a guide.

5 Tie the second cord's ends to the barrel clasp, keeping the section of small beads in the center. It should hang slightly lower than the pendant cord. Trim off the extra cord.

a ring for every finger

Now you can create playful rings quicker than you can say, "Let's craft."

HANGIN' OUT

It doesn't take many supplies to make rings! The pinkie rings on these pages just use beads and elastic, and they're...

seriously cool!

wrap ring (thumbs, pages 62-63)

WHAT YOU NEED

Strong glue, such as Krazy; memory wire for rings
  (available in crafts and bead stores)
End cap beads or round-nose pliers; assorted beads

HERE'S HOW

1 Use pliers to curl one end of the wire into a
  tiny loop, or use a small dab of glue on one
end of the wire and place an end cap bead. Let dry.

2 Place beads onto wire leaving a small space
  at the end. Use pliers to make another
loop, or add a dab of glue and the end cap. Let dry.

black-and-red ring
(pointer finger, page 62)

WHAT YOU NEED

Ruler; scissors; elastic cord; two-hole frame bead
Red accent bead; red and black seed beads

HERE'S HOW

1 Cut an 8-inch-long piece of elastic. Thread the
  elastic through the frame bead, stringing the
accent bead inside the frame.

2 String enough seed beads on each
  side of the frame bead to fit around
  your finger. Tie several knots; trim off excess.

heart ring
(pointer finger, page 63)

WHAT YOU NEED

Ruler; scissors; elastic cord; two-hole heart bead
Accent beads; seed beads

HERE'S HOW

1 Cut an 8-inch-long piece of elastic. Thread it
  through one side of the heart bead. Thread
on accent beads to fit inside the heart. Push the
elastic through the other hole in the heart.

2 String enough beads on each side of the
  heart bead to fit around your finger. Tie
several tight knots and trim off excess elastic.

red-and-blue ring
(middle finger, page 62)

WHAT YOU NEED

Ruler; scissors; elastic cord
Seed beads; decorative glass bead; bell cap

HERE'S HOW

1 Cut an 8-inch-long piece of elastic. Place a
  seed bead in the center of the elastic and pull
both ends through the glass bead and bell cap.

2 Thread the ends of the elastic with seed
  beads. Knot ends; trim off excess.

green and gold ring
(middle finger, page 63)

WHAT YOU NEED

Ruler; scissors; elastic cord; seed beads
Large bell cap with holes; accent bead to fit in cap

HERE'S HOW

1. Cut a 12-inch piece of elastic and weave it in and out of holes on bell cap, adding seed beads as you weave. Tie a knot; trim off excess.

2. Cut a 4-inch-long piece of elastic. Pull it through the accent bead and then through the holes on bell cap. Tie the elastic on the bottom.

3. Pull the elastic through the hole again and string on seed beads. Knot several times and trim off excess elastic.

silver bobble ring
(ring finger, page 62)

WHAT YOU NEED

Ruler; scissors; elastic cord
Two-hole silver accent bead; multicolor seed beads

HERE'S HOW

1. Cut an 8-inch piece of elastic. Thread one end through one set of holes in the two-hole bead.

2. String on enough seed beads to fit your finger. Knot the ends together. Repeat for the other set of holes. Trim off excess elastic.

pink and silver ring
(ring finger, page 63)

WHAT YOU NEED

Ruler; scissors; elastic cord
Pink accent bead; silver seed beads

HERE'S HOW

1. Cut an 8-inch-long piece of elastic. Place the accent bead in the center of the elastic.

2. String enough seed beads on both sides of the accent bead to fit around your finger twice. Knot ends and trim off excess elastic.

silver or gold rings
(pinky fingers, pages 62–63)

WHAT YOU NEED

Scissors; beading elastic; silver or gold beads

HERE'S HOW

1. Cut an 8-inch piece of elastic. Thread the elastic with enough beads to fit your finger. Knot the ends; trim off excess.

go-for-the-gold necklaces

hearts and triangles

WHAT YOU NEED

Cotton waxed bead cord in green, pale pink, and
bright pink; ruler; scissors

Gold outline charms with large beading holes in
heart and triangle shapes (available in bead stores)

HERE'S HOW

1 Cut a 32-inch-long piece of cord from each
cord color.

2 Hold the three cords together in one hand.
Thread on the center charm, positioning it
in the middle of the cords.

3 Tie a knot on
each side of the
charm while holding the
three strands of cord.

4 Tie knots
3/4 inches from
the first knot on each
side. For each side of the
necklace, thread on
another charm and tie
another knot; repeat until
the necklace is finished.

5 Decide how long
you want the
necklace, making sure it
can slip over your head.
Knot the ends together.
Trim off the extra cord.

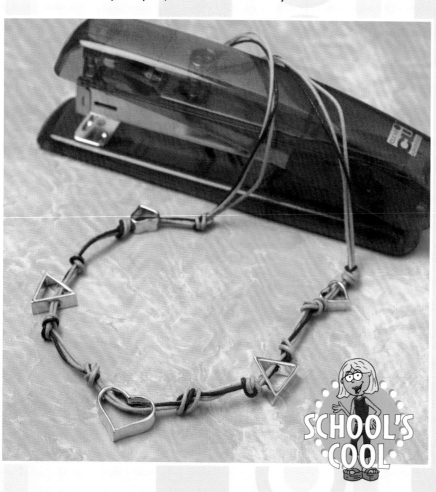

SCHOOL'S COOL

Gold charm shapes float on knotted lengths of color cord for a totally hip look.

HANGIN' OUT

so circular

WHAT YOU NEED

Green cotton waxed bead cord; ruler; scissors
2 small and 2 large gold circular charms with large
beading holes; 2 glass beads with large beading
holes to fit inside charms (available in bead stores)

HERE'S HOW

1 Cut a 12-inch-long piece of cord and two 30-inch-long pieces. Using the 12-inch piece, tie a knot at one end; place a small charm onto the cord. Tie a knot after the charm.

2 Tie a knot $1/2$ inch from the first. Thread the cord through the first hole of a large charm; place a bead on the cord before inserting it through the second hole in the charm. Tie a knot. Tie on another large charm with a bead and another small charm. Trim off the extra cord after the knot.

3 Insert a 30-inch piece of cord into one hole of each end charm. With the ends even, knot each cord close to the charm. For each side, hold the two strands together and tie knots in the cord.

4 Hold the cord ends together. Making sure the necklace can slip over your head, knot all four cords. Trim off extra.

stylin' sets

Use a medallion to create an ultracool necklace and make earrings and a headband to match!

SCHOOL'S COOL

Buy a medallion that fits your personality, find beads to match, and you can make a jewelry set that is ...

seriously cool

contemporary swirl set (page 68)

WHAT YOU NEED

for the necklace

Beading tray (see page 10) or felt; swirl pendant bead
Assorted beads in pairs; beading wire; scissors
16 silver disk spacer beads; barrel clasp; crimp beads
Small silver spacer beads for the
ends; crimping pliers

HERE'S HOW

1 Lay beads on the
beading tray, beginning at the
0 mark (center) with your pendant. Arrange the
beads up to the 9-inch mark on both sides in the
same pattern, including several small silver beads
on the ends.

2 Cut a 30-inch piece of beading wire. Put the
end of wire through a crimp bead, the barrel
clasp, and back through the crimp bead. Slide the
crimp bead next to the clasp. Crimp the bead with
crimping pliers until it smashes and won't move.

3 String on beads over both strands of wire
until all are strung. End with a crimp bead.

4 Put the end of wire through the barrel
clasp, then push back through the crimp
bead and other beads until you cannot see the
end. Crimp the bead with the pliers.

fish
hook
ear
wires

WHAT YOU NEED

for the earrings

Thin beading wire; scissors; fish hook ear wires
Seed beads; accent beads

HERE'S HOW

1 Cut two beading wires to the length you want
your earrings, plus an additional 2 inches.
With tails even, tie each onto the ear wire loops.

2 String seed beads and then accent beads
onto the wire. Wrap the ends of the wire
into the final beads several times to secure. Trim off
the extra wire. Shape the wires as you like them.

WHAT YOU NEED

for the headband

Needle and thread; stretch headband
7 silver disk spacer beads; 7 accent beads

HERE'S HOW

1 Thread the needle. Tie a knot at one end. From
the back side of the headband, sew on a
silver spacer, then an accent bead. Make several loops
of thread through the beads and back into the
headband. Sew six more pairs on the headband.

vintage-look medallion set
(page 69)

WHAT YOU NEED

for the necklace

Beading tray (see page 10) or felt; bronze-and-stone
  pendant bead; assorted beads, keeping in pairs
Disk and assorted spacer bronze beads; ruler
Small silver spacer beads for the ends; beading wire
Scissors; barrel clasp; crimp beads; crimping pliers

HERE'S HOW

1. Lay down beads on a beading board or felt in
   your own pattern or follow the pattern of
beads used here. Arrange the beads beginning at
the 0 mark (center) with your pendant. Arrange the
beads up to the 9-inch mark on both sides until you
have 18 inches of beads, including several small
silver beads on the ends.

2. Cut a piece of beading wire about 30 inches
   long. Place one end of the beading wire
into the barrel clasp and fold over the wire about
2 inches. Place the crimp bead over both ends of
the wire right next to the barrel clasp, then crimp
with the crimping pliers until the bead smashes and
won't move.

3. String on the beads over both strands of
   wire; continue stringing until all beads are
on the wire. The last bead should be a crimp bead.

4. Put the end of wire through the barrel
   clasp, then back through the crimp bead
and other beads. Crimp the bead with the pliers.

WHAT YOU NEED

for the earrings

Beading wire; ruler; scissors; fish hook ear wires
Small coordinating beads

HERE'S HOW

1. For each earring, cut wires 3 inches longer
   than the desired size of beaded loop. Tie one
end onto the loop at the bottom of the ear wire.

2. Place beads onto wire in any pattern you
   wish, then pull the end back through the
wire loop and tie it securely. Clip off extra wire.

WHAT YOU NEED

for the headband

Fabric-covered headband
Crafts glue; paintbrush; assorted small beads

HERE'S HOW

1. Brush a thick coat of glue onto the front of
   the headband. Sprinkle wet glue with
beads. Let dry.

dazzling purses

book-style purse (below)

WHAT YOU NEED

Papiér-mâché book form with opening lid (available in crafts stores)

Lime green acrylic paint; paintbrush

Pencil; crafts glue; seed beads

Crafts glue; gold glitter; newspaper

Sharp instrument for poking holes in cardboard, such as a phillips screwdriver

Beading wire; ruler; beads for handle

Scissors; crafting foam, such as Fun Foam

Strong adhesive, such as E6000; Velcro

HERE'S HOW

1 Paint book form inside and out with acrylic paint. Let dry. If a second coat is needed, let dry between coats.

2 Draw your initials on the front of the book.

3 Fill in each letter with a generous amount of glue. Sprinkle seed beads onto wet glue. Let dry. Shake off the loose beads.

SCHOOL'S COOL

72

You'll look like a fashion model when you carry a glamorous purse.

Paint the edges (the page ends) of the book with crafts glue. Sprinkle with gold glitter. Shake off onto newspaper and return the excess to your glitter container.

Have an adult help you use a phillips screwdriver or other pointed object to poke holes where you want handles to attach.

Open purse. Tie a bead very tightly to one end of a 30-inch piece of wire. Pull the wire from the inside of box, leaving the end anchor bead inside. String beads onto the handle to create your own pattern until you have the length that you want. Place the other end of the wire into the other hole, pulling it tightly. Place another anchor bead on the wire inside the box. Wrap the beading wire several times through the inside bead to secure it tightly. Trim off excess wire with scissors.

Cut a rectangular piece of crafting foam to make a strap that will fit from the back side to the front side. Use lots of adhesive to glue the back side of the strap to the back of book. Let dry.

continued on page 74

73

8. Glue a small piece of Velcro on the end of strap and onto the front side of the book.

box-style purse (page 73)

WHAT YOU NEED

Papiér mâché box with hinged lid; acrylic paint
Paintbrush; white glue; seed beads; 2 pipe cleaners
Sharp instrument for poking holes in cardboard
Large beads for handle and inside box
Stretchy headband or colored elastic; scissors

HERE'S HOW

1. Paint your box inside and out with acrylic paint. Let dry. You may have to paint two or three coats. Let it dry between coats.

2. Using the photo on page 73 as a guide, paint sections of box with lots of white glue.

3. Sprinkle seed beads into wet glue as shown in Photo A, opposite. Let dry. Shake off extra beads.

4. Have an adult help you use a phillips screwdriver or other pointed object to poke two holes in the lid where you want a handle attached. Poke one hole for the bead clasp on the front portion of the box as shown in Photo B.

5. To make the bead clasp, slide a large bead to the center of a pipe cleaner. Bend the ends together, and push it through the hole

made on the bottom portion of the box as shown in Photo C. Secure it with a bead on the inside, twisting the pipe cleaner until tight.

6. For the handle, tie a bead on one end of a pipe cleaner. Pull the pipe cleaner through the hole from the inside of the box to the outside.

7. Add the beads for the handle, as shown in Photo D, leaving enough room to secure the other end of the handle inside the box lid.

8. Put the other end of the pipe cleaner through the other handle hole and inside the lid; secure it with another bead.

9. Ask an adult to make two holes for the lid loop closure using a phillips screwdriver or

MOM KEEPS BORROWING MY PURSES TO SHOW OFF TO HER FRIENDS.

A **B**

C **D**

other pointed object. For the loop, cut a 5-inch-long piece of elastic headband or a decorative elastic piece. Insert each end through the holes. Thread a bead onto the elastic ends. Tie the ends into a knot, as shown in Photo E, leaving the loop long enough to hook over the large bead on the pipe cleaner.

E

colorful rings and things

Foot jewelry is "soooo" in, and these sets really rake in the compliments.

SCHOOL'S COOL

Wear these classy foot sets barefoot or with summery sandals to snag a look that is . . . *Seriously cool*

77

blue and silver set (page 76)

WHAT YOU NEED

10 decorative headpins
Assorted blue seed and other beads
Round-nose pliers
Tape; ruler
0.5 mm elastic bead cord
Scissors
Small silver spacer beads

HERE'S HOW

1. Assemble the dangles first. Place enough tiny beads on headpins to fill all but 1/4 inch of the top of pin.

2. Use round-nose pliers to bend a loop on the end of the headpin. Press together to hold securely.

3. Place a piece of tape on one end of a 15-inch-long piece of elastic. This will keep the beads from slipping off while you work.

4. You can create your own pattern of beads, alternating with spacers and the dangles you created. Place several beads, then a dangling headpin, then more beads until you have about 8 1/2 inches of elastic strung with beads. Tie the ends together in several secure knots, and trim off the excess cord.

5. For the toe ring, string seed beads and one accent bead onto a short piece of elastic until the desired size is reached. Tie several tight knots, and trim off the excess cord.

I'D BETTER GET A PEDICURE SO MY FEET LOOK AS NICE AS MY JEWELRY!

78

rainbow set (page 77)

WHAT YOU NEED

10 decorative headpins
Assorted colored large seed beads
Round-nose pliers
Tape; ruler
White beads; spacer beads
0.5 mm elastic bead cord
Scissors

HERE'S HOW

1 Assemble the dangles first. Place enough tiny beads onto headpins to fill all but 1/4 inch of the top of the pin.

2 Use round-nose pliers to bend a loop on the end of the headpin. Press together to hold securely.

3 Place a piece of tape on one end of a 15-inch piece of elastic. This will keep the beads from slipping off while you work.

4 You can create your own pattern of beads; or, place a white bead, a spacer, a dangler, a spacer, another white bead, and a spacer. Repeat the pattern until you have about 8 1/2 inches of elastic strung with beads.

5 Tie the ends together in several secure knots, and trim off the excess cord.

6 For the toe ring, string seed beads onto a short piece of elastic until you have about 1 inch of beads strung; wrap around toe for fit. Add or subtract beads if needed. Tie several tight knots, and trim off the excess.

INDEX

MY SILLY DAD NOW CALLS ME LIZZIE MCBEADER!